Life Cycle Costing

Arkie Fanning PE, CCE

31 March 2014

Table of Contents

1. Basics of Life cycle cost analysis

The components of a life cycle cost analysis vary from application to application. Basically one is trying to determine all of the factors that make up the cost of a particular alternative. The easiest way to demonstrate a life cycle is to show an example. Assume there are two alternatives that must be evaluated to determine the correct action to take. Table 1 shows the assumptions for each of the alternatives:

Table 1

Alternative A;
Life-	10	Years
Capital cost:	$100,000	
Annual energy cost:	$10,000	
Annual O&M cost:	$15,000	

Alternative B:
Life-	10	Years
Capital cost:	$150,000	
Annual energy cost:	$5,000	
Annual O&M cost:	$12,000	

This is a very simple example, just to show how to do a life cycle. For instance, the number of years shown in the example are the same for both alternatives, and this does not happen all of the time. Also, there is always a do nothing alternative (the do nothing alternative may not be feasible but it should always be considered) that must be examined and that is ignored for this example also. But this simple example will show you the purpose of a life cycle. That purpose, by the way, is to select the most cost advantageous alternative among many.

First, let's do a spreadsheet showing the cash flow for each alternative. This should make it easier to see what will be compared between these alternatives.

Table 2

Alternative A

Year	Capital Cost	Energy Cost	O&M Cost	Annual Cost
0	$100,000			$100,000
1		$10,000	$15,000	$25,000
2		$10,000	$15,000	$25,000
3		$10,000	$15,000	$25,000
4		$10,000	$15,000	$25,000
5		$10,000	$15,000	$25,000
6		$10,000	$15,000	$25,000
7		$10,000	$15,000	$25,000
8		$10,000	$15,000	$25,000
9		$10,000	$15,000	$25,000
10		$10,000	$15,000	$25,000
Total				$350,000

Alternative B

Year	Capital Cost	Energy Cost	O&M Cost	Annual Cost
0	$150,000			$150,000
1		$5,000	$12,000	$17,000
2		$5,000	$12,000	$17,000
3		$5,000	$12,000	$17,000
4		$5,000	$12,000	$17,000
5		$5,000	$12,000	$17,000

6	$5,000	$12,000	$17,000
7	$5,000	$12,000	$17,000
8	$5,000	$12,000	$17,000
9	$5,000	$12,000	$17,000
10	$5,000	$12,000	$17,000
Total			$320,000

So based on the two data sets which is the more attractive offer (in this case the least cost offer)?

If you said, I don't know, you said the right thing. Why don't we know yet? Because we still only have ½ the puzzle. We have the cost side but we do not have the valuation side. The valuation is set once we know the appropriate discount rate.

What is a discount rate? It is how we value our funds. This is easy to show for a homeowner, for instance, the value of the funds for the homeowner is his/her mortgage rate. That was the rate the homeowner agreed to in order to obtain the funds necessary to purchase his/her house.

So what is the appropriate discount rate for our example? I am going to assume this is a U.S. Government life cycle analysis. The Government defines the value of our funds based on econometric models. Each year the Government issues OMB (Office of Management and Budget) Circular A-94. This circular defines the appropriate discount rate to use. The current discount rate for a ten year analysis is:

Nominal rate for ten year analysis is 3.0%

Real rate for ten year analysis is 1.3%

(This was effective 10 Dec 2010)

So which rate should I use?

Well the rate depends upon the data gathered and the projection to be used. Simply put we use a nominal rate for any analysis that includes inflation. The real rate is used for any analysis that does not include inflation. Since we did not specify that the costs shown are in current or constant dollars (i.e. current includes inflation, constant does not), I will assume the data set is in constant dollars.

Now we can answer the question as to which of the alternatives are best:

Table 3

Alternative A						
	Capital	Energy	O&M	Annual		Present
Year	Cost	Cost	Cost	Cost	Discount	Worth
0	$100,000			$100,000	1.0000	$100,000
1		$10,000	$15,000	$25,000	0.9936	$24,839
2		$10,000	$15,000	$25,000	0.9808	$24,520
3		$10,000	$15,000	$25,000	0.9682	$24,206
4		$10,000	$15,000	$25,000	0.9558	$23,895
5		$10,000	$15,000	$25,000	0.9435	$23,588
6		$10,000	$15,000	$25,000	0.9314	$23,286
7		$10,000	$15,000	$25,000	0.9195	$22,987
8		$10,000	$15,000	$25,000	0.9077	$22,692
9		$10,000	$15,000	$25,000	0.8960	$22,401
10		$10,000	$15,000	$25,000	0.8845	$22,113
Total				$350,000		$334,526
Alternative B						
	Capital	Energy	O&M	Annual		Present

Year	Cost	Cost	Cost	Cost	Discount	Worth	
	$150,000			$150,000	1.0000	$150,000	
1		$5,000	$12,000	$17,000	0.9936	$16,891	
2		$5,000	$12,000	$17,000	0.9808	$16,674	
3		$5,000	$12,000	$17,000	0.9682	$16,460	
4		$5,000	$12,000	$17,000	0.9558	$16,249	
5		$5,000	$12,000	$17,000	0.9435	$16,040	
6		$5,000	$12,000	$17,000	0.9314	$15,834	
7		$5,000	$12,000	$17,000	0.9195	$15,631	
8		$5,000	$12,000	$17,000	0.9077	$15,430	
9		$5,000	$12,000	$17,000	0.8960	$15,232	
10		$5,000	$12,000	$17,000	0.8845	$15,037	
Total				$320,000		$309,478	

For this example the least expensive alternative is alternative B at $309 K. Alternative A comes in at $334 K.

This example shows that just because something is less expensive to start with (capital cost) it does not mean it is the best economic alternative. That is the essence of life cycle. We are determining the impact of all costs on our bottom line and not just the first or capital cost.

2. Important components of a Life Cycle.

A life cycle can be viewed as being made up of three components. The costs themselves (these are typically point estimates of the costs-more on that later), the discount rate (also called the time value of money component) and a sensitivity analysis.

We will take up the discussion of the discount rate in the next section. We will save the discussion of the sensitivity analysis for a much later time, just be aware, it is a part of every life cycle and if not done important information is not being provided to the decision makers.

The first of the components is the cost themselves. These costs are almost always estimates based on either expert judgment or from historical records. The costs are always the hardest part to determine. Just what were the XXX-you name it costs for this alternative.

There are also different kinds of costs and different ways that costs get absorbed into an accounting system. Just what goes into the life cycle based on all costs that are available is a difficult thing to judge sometimes. Basically, the life cycle cost engineer or analyst must determine what costs are appropriate and where to place them in the life cycle. Here is an example of something that could be a stumper.

A component should be replaced once every five years. The cost of replacement is $10,000. There is a sinking fund established that will pay for this. This fund expenses $2,000 per year to the budget for the replacement. At the end of five years, the component is purchased. As the life cycle engineer how would you represent this cash flow? Is it $2,000 per year or is it $10,000 in year 5? It does make a difference in your life cycle.

The easiest answer is to tie the cash flow to the actual expenditures. You may wish to account for some of the time value of the sinking fund (for instance if the sinking fund earns interest then the actual expenditure for the component will be less than $10 K) but you should show the cost when it actually occurs, in year 5. Your purpose is not to be an accountant but to determine the most effective use of funds for your company and/or Government.

Here are some of the types of costs you will have to deal with and some suggestions on how to handle those costs.

Capital costs-This is also called first cost. Usually it is shown as time 0 on your life cycle and it represents the start of the life cycle. There may be additional capital costs throughout your life cycle, and if so, then they should be shown in the year that they occur. There may be some residual value to the firm for the expenditure of this capital costs at the end of the life cycle. We will cover how to handle this situation when we discuss salvage costs.

Annual costs or continuous costs or variable costs-Many costs lend themselves to this category. Labor, energy use, water use, materials, these are all variable or semivariable costs, that is, it is close to a linear relationship between use and cost. For instance, if I use 2,000 KWH versus 3,000 KWH, I would typically pay the same cost per KWH. There are times when you will get quantity discounts. Just do the math and show them appropriately in your spreadsheet. The good thing about variable costs are that once you have an estimate of that variable cost it is easy to use that estimate by linear scaling for most possible scenarios under consideration.

Step costs-These are costs that act as a stair step. It goes from say $1,000 to $2,000 based on a usage. A good example of this is the concept of demand payments for electrical use. You will often pay a demand portion in your energy bill each month and this represents the amount of capacity of the electrical system you are using. Often, you will pay a demand of $/KW up to a certain amount and the very instant you cross that amount you will immediately pay the higher $/KW and it is often for a whole year.

Replacement costs-You will doubtless have situations where you have to replace equipment. There are three parts to a replacement cost. What is the cost, when will it be made and how long will the replacement last. Each part will be discussed later on and you will be showed how to represent replacement costs in your life cycle.

Energy or utility costs- These are electrical costs, water costs, propane costs-you name it. Basically, our rules represent energy costs as a different beast because they have a different inflation rate than non-energy costs. The Government has long recognized that energy costs are more variable than other costs and have provided different escalation rates for the different types of energy that you may encounter out in the real world.

Operations and maintenance costs-These are your day to day costs of running the office, plant, shop, etc. This cost represents the cost of the operator say of the machine that is being considered for replacement. This cost is often overlooked in life cycles, particularly the difference that may result from the various alternatives. If one alternative will reduce O&M costs, it should be represented in the life cycle even if the person that represents that O&M does not go away. The theory is that the person will be used for other work.

Sunk costs-These are costs that have already been expended and have no impact on the life cycle. That being said, decision makers are often clueless about this concept and they are also vested in past decisions. Telling them that the $100 K they spent last year to fix the problem is immaterial because the problem still exists does not sit well with them. Just be aware that you should not include them in your life cycle. If you do have to because of the situation you should always and I mean always do a sensitivity analysis showing the impact of not including them in the life cycle.

Opportunity costs- These are the costs that you pay for taking one alternative over another. Most life cycles will not be affected by opportunity costs but some that review the life cycle may ask what the opportunity costs are for the commitment for the funds. Tell them to get a life. The truth is, opportunity costs are not within the prevue of the life cycle, someone has already made a decision that they will pursue some course of action to fix some problem. That is the focus of the life cycle, the most economical way of fixing that problem. The person that made the decision to pursue the alternatives should have taken the opportunity costs into account.

Wash Costs-These are costs that are the same for all alternatives under consideration. An example would be if there is a single operator that will run whatever machine is decided upon by the life cycle decision. These costs are often not shown on a life cycle. I personally think they should be, to show them will not affect the decision (if A>B then A+C>B+C) even though it may reduce the percentage of the difference between the alternatives. I feel strongly they should be shown because decision makers will look for costs they recognize and if they do not see them they will question the analysis.

These are just some of the more obvious costs, there are many others you will encounter. Just remember that the purpose of the life cycle analysis is to represent the cash expenditures that impact the decision to be made. That means actual funds being spent in some way. Therefore, there are things that accountants include in their world that the life cycle will not include in its world. Also there are times when a cost will be represented (say depreciation) for some life cycles and it will not be represented in other life cycles. Always remember the purpose is to make the most cost effective decision. It is up to you as the engineer on the job to determine what the factors are that influence that decision.

3. The Discount Rate

    The discount rate is the most misunderstood concept in life cycle analysis. The purpose of the discount rate is to define the time value of the funds that will be used for the various alternatives in the life cycle. Even when specified by regulation (as it is for most Government life cycles) you should always do a sensitivity analysis on it. It has a great impact on the final decision and usually, no one knows, including economists, what the "right" discount rate is.

    Conventions of discount:

    There are several discounting conventions. Usually the convention chosen does not change the recommended decision. But it can on rare occasions. The accepted convention for Government life cycles is the mid-year convention. This is actually specified by OMB A-94. Most textbooks utilize the end of year convention for most of their analyses (at least the ones I've seen and utilized over my varied career) but it is important to utilize mid-year as the starting point. Just like any other parameter, you should do a sensitivity analysis on the discount rate.

    Here are the generally accepted discount conventions:

    Mid-year-The assumptions is that all cash flows occur at the middle of the year of your life cycle. If you have a January –

December life cycle then the assumption is that the cash flow for the costs are in July.

Middle of the year-This is close to the mid-year assumption and it was used a lot before personal computers became so prevalent. It takes beginning of the year discount and the end of the year discount, adds them together and divides by two. It is unnecessary these days because computers can easily handle power functions (which is required for mid-year).

Beginning of the year-This assumes all cash flows are on the first day of the year. I've rarely seen this in life cycles and you should investigate if someone has used it in one.

End of the year-This assumes all cash flows are on the last day of the year. It is used often (for instance your mortgage is doubtless based on an end of month cash flow concept).

How does one develop a discount rate?

There are often tables in finance, economics and engineering economics books that show the various values. Some computer programs have a built in discount factor function. But it is easy to build one on your own and I would recommend you do so in order to facilitate a later sensitivity analysis.

Let's assume the discount rate you want to determine is 5% per year. In other words, for some reason you are valuing your funds at 5% per year. The discount rate for this scenario becomes:

Mid-year: $d=i/(1+i)^{.5}$ therefore here is how you set it up

Table 4

Discount Rate
Mid-Year

Year		Uninverted Discount	5% Midyear Discount
	0	1.0000	1.0000
	1	1.0247	0.9759
	2	1.0759	0.9294
	3	1.1297	0.8852
	4	1.1862	0.8430
	5	1.2455	0.8029
	6	1.3078	0.7646
	7	1.3732	0.7282
	8	1.4418	0.6936
	9	1.5139	0.6605
	10	1.5896	0.6291

Before you say "HUH!" let me show you how this is done.

Year 0= 1 there is no discount because that starts the time period for the life cycle.
Year 1 = Uninverted discount = $1.05^{.5}=1.0247$, discount = $1/1.0247=0.9759$
Tear 2= Univerted discount=$1.0247*1.05 = 1.0759$, discount = $1/1.0759=0.9294$
Etc.

This is easy to do on a computer and I would advise you set up a dummy cell for your discount value. That will make it easier to do your sensitivity analysis.

Table 5
End of year discount:

Discount Rate

End of year

Year	Uninverted Discount	5% End of Year Discount
0	1.0000	1.0000
1	1.0500	0.9524
2	1.1025	0.9070
3	1.1576	0.8638
4	1.2155	0.8227
5	1.2763	0.7835
6	1.3401	0.7462
7	1.4071	0.7107
8	1.4775	0.6768
9	1.5513	0.6446
10	1.6289	0.6139

It is easier to see the compounding with end of year discount (and that is probably why it is used so often) but it does understate the impact of the various costs you experience. Here is how you build up this spread sheet

Year 0 = Uninverted discount rate = 1, discount = 1/1 = 1
Year 1= Uninverted discount rate = 1 * 1.05 = 1.05, discount rate = 1/1.05 = 0.9524
Year 2= Uninverted discount rate = 1.05*1.05 = 1.1025, discount rate = 1/1.1025 = 0.9070
Etc.

Beginning of year assumes that there is no year 0. All cash flows start at year 1. Therefore the first cost and the annual cost for the first year are all evaluated as 1 for the first year. Other than that it is the same as the end of year. Here is what a beginning of the year discount rate looks like.

Table 6

Discount Rate
Beginning of Year

Year		Uninverted Discount	5% Begin of year Discount
	1	1.0000	1.0000
	2	1.0500	0.9524
	3	1.1025	0.9070
	4	1.1576	0.8638
	5	1.2155	0.8227
	6	1.2763	0.7835
	7	1.3401	0.7462
	8	1.4071	0.7107
	9	1.4775	0.6768
	10	1.5513	0.6446
	11	1.6289	0.6139

Again you should question the use of the beginning of the year discount convention. It does typically understate the first cost (relatively speaking of course, which is what a life cycle is all about the relative difference between the two alternatives).

Finally there is the middle of the year discount convention for year 1.

Table 7

Discount Rate
Middle of the year

Year		End of year Discount	5% middle of year Discount
	0	1.0000	1.0000
	1	0.9524	1.0500
Total		1.9524	0.9762

Here is how you get the value for year 1, you add the year 0 end of year discount (1.000) to the year 1 end of year discount (0.9524) to get 1.9524 then divide by 2, and you get 0.9762.

Here is a table showing middle of the year discount, if you compare to midyear you will see the rates are very similar and since midyear is easier to calculate (and more accurate in my opinion) you can see why very few people use middle of the year anymore.

Table 8

Discount Rate
Middle of the year
Year

Year	5% Middle of year discount
0	1.0000
1	0.9762
2	0.9297
3	0.8854
4	0.8433
5	0.8031
6	0.7649
7	0.7284
8	0.6938
9	0.6607
10	0.6293

4. Understanding the time value of money

The key to understanding life cycle cost is the understanding of the time value of money. Money has value that one can either spend or save. If one saves the money now in some sort of an investment, the anticipation is that there will be more money in the future. This is the time value of money in its simplest form.

This is the equation that can be used to determine the value tomorrow of what is not spent today.

$FV = P(1+i)^{k}$ Where

FV = Future Value
P = Present Value
n= number of periods (usually years)
i = Interest rate

Here is an example of how money will grow overtime.

Assume the at P = $10,000
n= 10 years
i = 6% per year

Table 9

Year		Start	Interest at 6%	End
	1	$10,000	$600	$10,600
	2	$10,600	$636	$11,236
	3	$11,236	$674	$11,910
	4	$11,910	$715	$12,625
	5	$12,625	$757	$13,382
	6	$13,382	$803	$14,185
	7	$14,185	$851	$15,036
	8	$15,036	$902	$15,938
	9	$15,938	$956	$16,895
	10	$16,895	$1,014	$17,908

You would get the same value by directly applying the equation:

FV = $10,000 * (1=.06)^10 = $17,908

The table illustrates the compounding effect. This compounding is what makes investments over time powerful and the reason I showed the table is I wanted to show the compounding effect. Notice that at the end of each period (year in this example but it is typically daily or monthly) the value of the interest is added. The next period you earn interest on not only the original investment ($10,000) but also on the interest that accrued from the period before.

The idea of discounting is basically just taking the time value of money and putting it in reverse.

One multiplies by the inverse of the interest and therefore determines the time value of the funds flows at this point in time.

I liked to look at a life cycle by putting all costs into time buckets. This is similar to the cost diagrams you see in many engineering economic textbooks that show all expenditures on a line with an arrow pointing in the appropriate direction and with the magnitude of the arrow dependent upon the value of the expenditure. If you feel comfortable drawing cash flow diagrams, please do. I never have, I prefer to work directly on a computer and put everything in time buckets. Here is what I mean.

At time 0 you have the first cost-seldom if ever do you have anything else but first cost at time 0 (or capital cost) but if you do then just put it in another category at time 0. Here is the start of the spreadsheet.

Time bucket Concept

	First	Misc
Time period	Cost	Cost
0	$10,000	$100

So for time period 0, I have an expenditure of $10,100.

At time period one I experience my first variable costs. Let's say energy costs of $500 per year for the first year and O&M cost of $600 per year for the first year. This costs will repeat (I will do this as a constant dollar analysis-don't worry we will get to current dollar analysis and show how to handle inflation) for each year of my life cycle (I will assume a 5 year life cycle), now my spreadsheet looks like this.

Table 10

Time bucket Concept					
	First	Misc		Energy	O&M
Time period	Cost	Cost		Costs	Costs
0	$10,000		$100	$0	$0
1				$500	$600
2				$500	$600
3				$500	$600
4				$500	$600
5				$500	$600

Now I have defined my time periods 1-5 and have showed the costs that accrue to them. I have determined there are no other costs. I have also determined that my discount rate is 3% and that I will use a mid-year discounting convention to determine the value of my life cycle. I can now complete the life cycle and show the time value of all these expenditures at time 0 (when the decision is made to select an alternative).

Table 11

Time bucket Concept							
	First	Misc	Energy	O&M	Cash		Present
Time period	Cost	Cost	Costs	Costs	Flow	Disc	Worth
0	$10,000	$100	$0	$0	$10,100	1.0000	$10,100
1	$0	$0	$500	$600	$1,100	0.9853	$1,084
2	$0	$0	$500	$600	$1,100	0.9566	$1,052
3	$0	$0	$500	$600	$1,100	0.9288	$1,022
4	$0	$0	$500	$600	$1,100	0.9017	$992
5	$0	$0	$500	$600	$1,100	0.8755	$963
							$15,213

All of this data gathering and analysis has been completed just to get to the bottom line present worth (also known as present value) of $15,213. So what is so important about this present worth? It isn't like one can spend a present worth dollar.

Present worth (or future worth if you want to reverse the calculation) is the value of this cash stream at time 0, the time the decision will be made. If I have performed my job correctly, I will be able to compare different alternatives with different cash flows and show the one that is the more cost effective (least costly in this instance but with the proper spreadsheet it could be best return on investment or some other measure). This allows the decision maker to know where to put their resources to get the best return and also allows for a full accounting of costs for each alternative.

Compounding is the reverse of discounting. Most people understand compounding (put something in the bank, let it ride, you get more out eventually). Here is the equation for compound interest (based on a year as the time line):

F = P(1+r/n)^nt

Where:

F= Future Value
P = Present Value
r = Interest rate
n = Number of times per year the investment is compounded
t = Number of years invested

Here is an example:

Let P = $1,000

r = .06 per annum (6% per year)

n = 4 times per year (quarterly compounding)

t = 2 years

P =	$1,000.00	
r =	0.06	
n =	4	
t =	2	
r/n =	0.015	0.06/4
(1+r/n) =	1.015	
nt =	8	4*2=8
(1+r/n)^nt =	1.126493	
F =		
P(1+r/n)^nt=	$1,126.49	

You will often hear the term ieffective, which means what is the effective annual interest rate that I am paying or earning. In the previous example, substitute 1 for 2 in t, and you will have the ieffective rate (or APR-Annual Percentage Rate).

$(1+r/n)^{nt} =$ 1.061364

Ieffective = 1.061364-1 = .061364 = 6.13%

In this example, the compounding of the interest rate provides you with a 6.13% APR.

Someone once asked me what was the maximum number of times you can compound during a year. The answer is given by the continuous compound interest equation. It assumes that funds are compounded continually from the time put into the account. What impact does that have on the APR? Well here's the equation and an example showing the impact:

$F = P e^{rt}$ where

F= Future value

P = Present value

e = 2.718 (e is one of those magic constants that is used in many engineering and financial calculations-it is the basis for the natural logs and was actually discovered by Jacob Bernoulli when he was trying to determine the impact of continuous compounding of interest-it is used in many other calculations now)

r = interest rate

t = number of years invested

The value one gets for 6% continuous compounding is:

P = $1,000.00

e =	2.7182818
r =	0.06
t =	1
e^rt=	1.0618365
F = P(e^rt)	$1,061.84
ieff =	6.18% e^rt-1

So the difference in compounding instantly and always versus compounding quarterly for a 6% interest rate is 6.18%-6.13% = 0.05% or 0.0005. The difference per one thousand dollars in one year is $1061.84-

$1061.30= $0.54.

Continuous compounding is better than quarterly or weekly or daily compounding, but not by much.

Another useful equation is how to determine the balance remaining of a cash stream. This will be very important later when we discuss various return on investment, equity, and other associated financial ratios. Here is the equation. I will also show you how to do it on a spreadsheet so that you don't have to remember this equation.

$$B=A(1+r/n)^{nt}-P[\{(1+r/n)^{nt}-1\}/\{(1+r/n)-1\}]$$

Where B = Balance after t years

A = Amount Borrowed

P = Payment (does not include anything but interest and capital recovery)

r = interest rate

n=number of payments per year

t = number of years

I had to look this up on line in order to provide it to you. The truth is that one can determine the balance much easier when you use a spreadsheet than you can by using this equation. Here's how:

Assume I borrowed $100,000

The interest rate is 6% per annum

I make my payment 12 times per year (monthly)

I have a 5 year payment stream

What is my balance in say year 3 month 1?

Just use a spreadsheet to determine instead of utilizing the equations that I have shown. For instance the excel spreadsheet has the Payment Function =PMT(rate,nper,PV) which means you give it the interest rate, the number of pay periods and the Present value which is equal to the amount borrowed in the equation above.

Set up your spreadsheet this way:

Beginning Balance, Payment, Interest, Capital Recovery, Ending Balance

Beginning Balance = $100,000

Payment = PMT(.06/12,60,$100,000)=$1933.28

Interest = .06/12*$100,000 = $500.00

Capital Recovery = $1933.28-$500 = $1433.28

Ending balance = Beginning Balance-Capital recovery = $98,567

Now the key to making it easy is to ensure that your beginning balance for payment 2 is equal to the ending balance of Payment 1.

Now you just have to copy through 60 cells of your spreadsheet

The last cell should equal $0. If it does you have done your job right.

Here is the spreadsheet and look at the ending balance for payment 37 (year 3 payment 1-$41,905) to see what your balance is for the question asked earlier.

Table 12

Payment	Beginning Balance	Payment	Interest	Capital Recovery	Ending Balance
1	$100,000	$1,933	$500	$1,433	$98,567
2	$98,567	$1,933	$493	$1,440	$97,126
3	$97,126	$1,933	$486	$1,448	$95,679
4	$95,679	$1,933	$478	$1,455	$94,224
5	$94,224	$1,933	$471	$1,462	$92,762
6	$92,762	$1,933	$464	$1,469	$91,292
7	$91,292	$1,933	$456	$1,477	$89,815
8	$89,815	$1,933	$449	$1,484	$88,331
9	$88,331	$1,933	$442	$1,492	$86,839
10	$86,839	$1,933	$434	$1,499	$85,340
11	$85,340	$1,933	$427	$1,507	$83,834
12	$83,834	$1,933	$419	$1,514	$82,320
13	$82,320	$1,933	$412	$1,522	$80,798
14	$80,798	$1,933	$404	$1,529	$79,269
15	$79,269	$1,933	$396	$1,537	$77,732
16	$77,732	$1,933	$389	$1,545	$76,187
17	$76,187	$1,933	$381	$1,552	$74,635
18	$74,635	$1,933	$373	$1,560	$73,075
19	$73,075	$1,933	$365	$1,568	$71,507
20	$71,507	$1,933	$358	$1,576	$69,931
21	$69,931	$1,933	$350	$1,584	$68,347
22	$68,347	$1,933	$342	$1,592	$66,756

23	$66,756	$1,933	$334	$1,600	$65,156
24	$65,156	$1,933	$326	$1,607	$63,549
25	$63,549	$1,933	$318	$1,616	$61,933
26	$61,933	$1,933	$310	$1,624	$60,310
27	$60,310	$1,933	$302	$1,632	$58,678
28	$58,678	$1,933	$293	$1,640	$57,038
29	$57,038	$1,933	$285	$1,648	$55,390
30	$55,390	$1,933	$277	$1,656	$53,734
31	$53,734	$1,933	$269	$1,665	$52,069
32	$52,069	$1,933	$260	$1,673	$50,396
33	$50,396	$1,933	$252	$1,681	$48,715
34	$48,715	$1,933	$244	$1,690	$47,025
35	$47,025	$1,933	$235	$1,698	$45,327
36	$45,327	$1,933	$227	$1,707	$43,620
37	$43,620	$1,933	$218	$1,715	$41,905
38	$41,905	$1,933	$210	$1,724	$40,181
39	$40,181	$1,933	$201	$1,732	$38,449
40	$38,449	$1,933	$192	$1,741	$36,708
41	$36,708	$1,933	$184	$1,750	$34,958
42	$34,958	$1,933	$175	$1,758	$33,200
43	$33,200	$1,933	$166	$1,767	$31,432
44	$31,432	$1,933	$157	$1,776	$29,656
45	$29,656	$1,933	$148	$1,785	$27,871
46	$27,871	$1,933	$139	$1,794	$26,077
47	$26,077	$1,933	$130	$1,803	$24,275
48	$24,275	$1,933	$121	$1,812	$22,463
49	$22,463	$1,933	$112	$1,821	$20,642
50	$20,642	$1,933	$103	$1,830	$18,812
51	$18,812	$1,933	$94	$1,839	$16,972
52	$16,972	$1,933	$85	$1,848	$15,124
53	$15,124	$1,933	$76	$1,858	$13,266
54	$13,266	$1,933	$66	$1,867	$11,399
55	$11,399	$1,933	$57	$1,876	$9,523
56	$9,523	$1,933	$48	$1,886	$7,637
57	$7,637	$1,933	$38	$1,895	$5,742
58	$5,742	$1,933	$29	$1,905	$3,838

| 59 | $3,838 | $1,933 | $19 | $1,914 | $1,924 |
| 60 | $1,924 | $1,933 | $10 | $1,924 | $0 |

One more useful equation is the equation that shows the monthly payment for a given amortization schedule. To amortize something means to pay it off over time. Here is the monthly payment equation.

$C= rP/(1-[1+r]^{-n})$

Where

C = Monthly payment

r = interest rate per month

P = Amount borrowed (principle)

n = number of payments

So what is the cost of a monthly mortgage for a $200K house over 30 years (excluding taxes and insurance)at 6% per year?

r= .06/12 =.005

n = 30*12 =360

$C = .005*200,000/(1-[1+.005]^{-360}) = \$1,199.10$

Here it is broken out on a spreadsheet (which is what I like to do with long equations in order to trouble shoot the equation if I have made a mistake):

By the numbers
$C = rP/[1-(1+r)^{-n}\}$

P = $200,000
r =   0.005   .06/12

1+ r =	1.005	
n =	360	12*30
(1+r)^-n	0.166042	
1- (1+r)^-n		
=	0.833958	Call this X
r* P =	$1,000	
C =(r*P)/X	$1,199	Per month

You get the very same value if you just use the PMT function in Excell, but now you know where that function comes from.

5. Probabilistic evaluation of a cost proposal

There are a number of ways to evaluate a cost proposal. The way used most often is to determine the life cycle cost of the alternatives and make our decision based solely on cost effectiveness. But there are many other ways of evaluation that you as a cost engineer/analyst should know about.

There is a whole discipline of engineering dedicated to optimization (best decision given multiple criteria) theory. The field is known as Management Science, Operations Research, Decision Engineering, and sometimes it is inherent in the meaning of Systems Engineering. The purpose of this field of engineering is to make the best decision that can be made based on all of the information available.

The reason you should know about these methods is that in the future (at least I believe this will be the case) the cost community will be utilizing ranges instead of point values to make their decisions. You may have already seen some evidence of this. You may get a 90% confidence interval for instance saying that the cost is somewhere between $10,000 and $80,000.

One of the most often used method in determining the best decision is to use some form of expected value. The formal definition of expected value (or **expectation**, or **mathematical expectation**, or **mean**, or the **first moment**) of a random variable is the weighted average of all possible values that this random variable can take on. The weights used in computing this average correspond to the probabilities in case of a discrete random variable, or densities in case of continuous variables.

Like most things mathematical it is easier to show than to explain.

Since I really like tables I put together a table illustrating a simple expected value. I chose a discrete distribution and defined the probabilities. The probabilities always have to equal 100%.
Table 13

Expected Value

Value	Probability	Expected Value
$100,000	0.1	$10,000
$200,000	0.2	$40,000
$300,000	0.3	$90,000
$400,000	0.3	$120,000
$500,000	0.1	$50,000
	1	$310,000

Here is how this works. The first value is $100,000 is multiplied by 0.1 (10%) to get $10,000. Continue this process and you get the total final value of $310 K.

What this is saying is that the costs are ill defined and that via some mechanism we have developed the costs (values) and probabilities shown.

6. Ways of determining the advisability of an investment:
    Payback
    Savings to investment Ratio (SIR)
    Internal Rate of Return

The three main ways that I have seen in my career on how to determine the advisability of an investment outside of net present value is the use of payback, Savings to Investment Ratio and Internal Rate of Return. All three have their uses and all three can be used to separate the few from the many. This section will show you how to calculate each of these three measures.

Payback: Payback is simplicity itself, it asks the question, when do I get my money back (not turn a profit mind you, just when do I get my money back) on this investment. Well here is how you determine that.

Guess what, you set up a spreadsheet. Imagine that!

Assume the following:
Table 14

Payback

Year	Cost	Return	Flow	Cumulative
0	($10,000)		($10,000)	($10,000)
1		$4,000	$4,000	($6,000)

2	$4,000	$4,000	(2,000)
3	$4,000	$4,000	2,000
4	$4,000	$4,000	6,000
5	$4,000	$4,000	10,000

Payback

| = | $10,000 | $4,000 | 2.5 |

So the payback for this investment is 2.5 years.

A more sophisticated use of payback is the discounted payback. When you use the discounted payback you are taking into account the time value of the funds. Assume you have a 10% midyear discount. Now here is the spreadsheet for the discounted payback:

Table 15

Discounted Payback					Present	
Year	Cost	Return	Flow	Disc	Value	Cumulative
0	($10,000)		($10,000)	1.0000	($10,000)	($10,000)
1		$4,000	$4,000	0.9535	$3,814	($6,186)
2		$4,000	$4,000	0.8668	$3,467	($2,719)
3		$4,000	$4,000	0.7880	$3,152	$433
4		$4,000	$4,000	0.7164	$2,865	$3,298
5		$4,000	$4,000	0.6512	$2,605	$5,903

You see that the payback is further along in year 3 than in our other calculation. You can find out the approximate value by just using interpolation. There are 12 months in a year and the total for the year is $433 (cumulative) and $3,152 present value, so the point in the year when you go positive is $433/$3152 = 13.74%. 12 months * (1-13.74%) = 10.35 so the discounted payback period is approximately 2 years and 10.35 months. To do it exactly requires a lot more spreadsheet analysis and I've not seen an easy to use equation that shows it to you (though one may exist).

The reason it is advantageous to use the discounted payback is that you really need to ensure you are accounting for your cost of funds. If you don't you may be making a poor decision. That being said, a lot of companies do use the undiscounted payback as a screening mechanism and as long as it is not the final determination of where to put your scarce funds there is no problem with that.

Savings to investment ratios are used a lot in economic analysis to determine a quick and dirty answer as to whether to select an alternative. The calculation may be either discounted (preferred) or nondiscounted. If it is a discounted calculation and the SIR is greater than 1 then you know that the savings are greater than the cost. If they are undiscounted you do not have the same guarantee, however, undiscounted SIRs can be a useful tool to screen projects, particularly if the personnel developing the SIRs are not very familiar with life cycle costing techniques.

Here is the Savings to Investment Ratio discounted methodology:

Table 16

Savings to investment Ratio:
Assume a hurdle rate or discount rate of 10% midyear

Year	Investment	Return on inv	discount	NPV cost	NPV return
0	$100,000		1	$100,000	
1		$30,000	0.953463		$28,604
2		$30,000	0.866784		$26,004
3		$30,000	0.787986		$23,640

4	$30,000	0.716351	$21,491
5	$30,000	0.651228	$19,537
		$100,000	$119,274
	SIR:	119.27%	
	Conclusion-pursue		

Let's break this down and see what it is telling us:

First-our investment cost is $100K

Second: We have a hurdle rate (also called a required return rate) of 10% for our investments

Third: We believe our return will be $30,000 per year for our investment

Fourth: The discounted value of the return is divided by the discounted value of the cost

($119,724/$100,000) to get a value of 119.27% or 1.1927. We pursue anything >1.

The undiscounted SIR for this investment is $150,000/$100,000 = 1.5. Since it is undiscounted we do not know if we should pursue right away, but assume we are looking at many different projects and all have undiscounted SIRs. Then we can compare and determine which is the better course of action.

Of course all of this depends on our being able to accurately predict the costs and the returns, which we usually cannot do, but a business must have some method of determining where to place their investments, and this way, even if flawed, at least provides some logic that can be relied upon in the decision making process.

A related measure and one that is used a lot in corporate America is the Internal Rate of Return (IRR). This is defined as the annualized effective compounded return rate for an investment and also as the discount rate that makes the Net Present Value of All cash flows equal to zero. Be aware that if you use the IRR function in some software programs you can get both a positive and a negative IRR if there are multiple changes in cash flow (i.e. some years are positive cash flow and some are negative). You want the positive IRR or better yet, just do the math yourself. Here is how you determine an IRR for a project with these assumptions:

Table 17

Internal Rate of Return example

Assumptions:

Year	Costs
0	$20,000
5	$12,000
10	$7,000

Returns:
Years
1-10 $8,000   PER YEAR
Combined Costs and Returns

Year	Cost	Returns	Cash Flow	Disc	Present Worth
0	($20,000)		$0 ($20,000)	1.0000	($20,000)
1			$8,000 $8,000	0.8459	$6,767
2			$8,000 $8,000	0.6053	$4,842
3			$8,000 $8,000	0.4331	$3,465
4			$8,000 $8,000	0.3099	$2,479
5	($12,000)		$8,000 ($4,000)	0.2217	($887)
6			$8,000 $8,000	0.1587	$1,269

7		$8,000	$8,000	0.1135	$908
8		$8,000	$8,000	0.0812	$650
9		$8,000	$8,000	0.0581	$465
10	($7,000)	$8,000	$1,000	0.0416	$416
					$0
				Mid	
End of year			32%	year	40%

So if we use the end of year convention we get a 32% IRR for this cash flow example. If we use mid year convention we get 40% IRR for this cash flow example. In other words if someone offers you this opportunity, take it and run. But how did I accomplish this? Well I cheated on the end of year and used the IRR function in the spreadsheet I was using. But for the midyear I set up a dummy variable in my spreadsheet that controlled my discount rates and then just drove that to the discount rate that zeroed out the cash flows. Here is the dummy spread sheet column:

Table 18

Uninv
Disc
0.39755
1
1.18218
1.652156
2.308971
3.226902
4.509757
6.30261
8.808213
12.30992
17.20373
24.04307

As you can see the real value for the mid year is 0.39755 and not the 0.40 I rounded to. The steps are as follows:

Set up a dummy column that I call Univerted discount. For this case the year 0 value is 1 (this is always the case), year 1 is $1*1.39755^{.5} = 1.18218$, for year 2 the value is $1.39755*1.18218 = 1.65216$, and follow that protocol until you hit year ten.

In the discount column you divide 1 by the uninverted discount rate and this gets you the discount rate. For example:

Year 0 $= 1/1 = 1$

Year 1= $1/1.18218 = 0.8459$

The final discount column looks like this:

Table 19

Disc
1.0000
0.8459
0.6053
0.4331
0.3099
0.2217
0.1587
0.1135
0.0812
0.0581
0.0416

So what you do is manipulate your dummy variable until the discounted cash flows equal 0.

I would advise caution in using the IRR. It assumes you will earn the IRR percentage on that money for the whole time of the investment. This is seldom the case but still just like the SIR calculation (or payback or any of a host of other analysis tools) it can be very useful as a screening tool to identify those alternatives that are the best, at least given your assumptions.

One final note on IRR-you will sometimes see the term MARR-Minimum Attractive Rate of Return. This is essentially a preselected IRR that is used as a firm's hurdle rate. The hurdle rate is the minimum rate the investment must earn in order for the firm to be interested in pursuing that alternative.

7.   Depreciation

If you do mostly Government life cycles you will seldom have to worry with depreciation. However you should know it exists and know some of the more salient factors about depreciation. Depreciation is the reduction in value of an asset due to time and/or usage. It is important because depreciation reduces taxes, and in the non-Governmental world decisions are made based on after-tax profit. Since the Government does not pay taxes then we don't usually have to worry about depreciation, but sometimes we do, for instance if we are trying to determine what is in the taxpayers best interest when we are doing make versus buy life cycles. There are many different ways of accounting for depreciation and I refer you to any of a number of accounting or finance books for a more indepth analysis. The ones most common are MACRS, declining balance, and units of production (at least my experience tells me these are the most common but that is definitely not a statement I can back up with any statistics).

MACRS is the Modified Accelerated Cost Recovery System and is the method required by the Internal Revenue Service on a wide range of depreciable items. The declining balance method comes in many flavors (single declining and double declining being the most popular). The units of production method is favored in a lot of manufacturing situations. Just be aware that there are many ways of doing depreciation, and don't think that the straight line method taught in most textbooks is used very often, it is not, it is just easy to calculate.

What you need to know is that depreciation reduces cash flow. Reduced cash flow results in fewer taxes. Fewer taxes results in a higher after tax profit.

Here is an example. I used MACRS for a truck to show how this works.

A truck is viewed as a 5 year asset with depreciation over 6 years. The depreciation per year allowable is:

Table 20

MACRS-Example

Year	Depreciation
1	20.00%
2	32.00%
3	19.20%
4	11.52%
5	11.52%
6	5.76%

Assume the truck costs $20,000. Then the depreciable amount becomes:

Table 21

MACRS-Example

Year	Depreciation	$20,000 Truck Depr
1	20.00%	$4,000
2	32.00%	$6,400
3	19.20%	$3,840
4	11.52%	$2,304
5	11.52%	$2,304
6	5.76%	$1,152
		$20,000

If we assume the effective tax rate of the firm is 30% then we have the following:

MACRS-Example

Tax Rate		30.00%	$20,000	Tax
Year		Depreciation	Truck Depr	Savings
	1	20.00%	$4,000	$1,200
	2	32.00%	$6,400	$1,920
	3	19.20%	$3,840	$1,152
	4	11.52%	$2,304	$691
	5	11.52%	$2,304	$691
	6	5.76%	$1,152	$346
			$20,000	$6,000

Thus depreciation has reduced our tax bill by $1,200 in year one, etc. This is why depreciation is important. It increases the cash flow to the business and increases the after tax profit, and profit is one of the main goals of any firm.

8. Learning Curves

What are learning curves and what have they got to do with life cycle analysis? Well a learning curve or an improvement curve is a mathematical way of modeling increases in efficiency. It is a basic fact that people become more efficient at performing a task as they get experience with performing a task. There are a number of ways of modeling this, and the truth is the only way to really understand for any given instance is to study what is going on and determine what the relationship is between time and efficiency. Of course, this is a problem when you are doing projections and typically life cycles are projections. So we typically rely on a projection and if it is contractual then the contractor relies on that projection also and the truth is what it is, sometimes it will break for one party and sometimes for the other.

An accepted way of determining the improvement in unit production is called the cumulative average unit production (there is also a unit production model that uses this same general method and it is more widespread, however, you have to use midpoints to do a decent projection and that is beyond the scope of this article). The cumulative average model is shown as:

$Y = A X^b$

Where: Y = Cumulative Average unit cost
A = First unit cost
X = Unit
b = learning curve percentage which is log (b)/log 2

Here is an example:

Assume the following:

A =	$1,000
X =	5
b % =	0.9
log b % =	-0.0458
log 2 =	0.3010
b =	-0.1520
Y =	$783

So now that I have the numbers what do they mean? Here it the explanation:

A = First unit cost = $1,000

If you are very lucky you know this value. By knowing this value you can make accurate predictions of the future, unfortunately we seldom do know this value. At any rate, agree to it contractually or do some math to come up with the value (if you have several data sets of unit costs you can do a regression, you can also do some basic algebra to get the value assuming you have the data sets, usually of course you don't) because it is necessary to have a value in order to project the values in the future.

X = 5, this is the fifth unit of production

b = .90 that means we think we have a 90% learning curve going on, values of .8-.9 are typical in many industries where there is a lot of assembly.

Log b% is the logarithm of 0.90 = -0.0458

Log 2 = logarithm of 2 = 0.3010

b = -0.0458/0.3010 = -0.152

Y = $783 = $1,000*5^-0.152

This is the cumulative average interpretation of the curve which means the following:

The cumulative average for all 5 units is $783 therefore the total cost for the five units is:

5*$783 = $3,915

Had this been a unit cost curve (which is used more at least in my experience) then you would have either had to do the same calculation for 5 units or else do a midpoint. The mathematics is not hard for a midpoint, however I just want you to be aware of the fact that learning curve exists, if you wish to know more there are many books that cover this in much more detail than this.

Here would be the values if we were using the unit cost version of this model:

Table 22

Y	X		A	b
$1,000.00		1	$1,000	-0.1520
$900.00		2	$1,000	-0.1520
$846.21		3	$1,000	-0.1520
$810.00		4	$1,000	-0.1520
$782.99		5	$1,000	-0.1520
$4,339.19				

Avg $867.84

As you can see the difference is $4,339-$3,915 = $424. If there is confusion between you and the contractor on whether a unit curve or cumulative average is what is appropriate, you can either fall back on the contract or do some basic math and covert one to the other. The conversion is not that difficult but again it is outside the scope of this article.

One thing about learning curves and the construction industry, I have been involved in construction cost estimating off and on for a lot of years. I have yet to see a learning curve used. The logic employed is that the methods of construction are universal and therefore the learning curve has already been established and the average is what we expect in most instances. While I do not always accept this logic I usually do not push the point because most of the personnel involved in construction have never even heard of a learning curve. If you are in the construction industry just be aware that this does exist and if you have an instance when you are doing, in effect, multiple units of the same item, you may wish to see if a learning curve can be employed in modeling the cost of the nth unit.

9. Linear Regression

Linear regression-isn't that statistics? What is it doing in a book on life cycle cost?

Yes, linear regression is statistics, however, it is used extensively in forecasting of costs and therefore in life cycle analysis. It is a very simple form of statistics and it is fairly accurate (robust is what the statisticians say) in most instances. Linear regression models one variable "y" in terms of another variable "x". The assumption is you know x very well and y not so well, so you are going to determine the unknown y from the known x. It may sound complex but it isn't. Here is an example of what I have found to be the most used form of linear regression:

$$Y = A + B X$$

Where: Y = The cost of the Xth unit

A = Fixed cost that doesn't change with the number of units

B = The variable cost per unit

X = Number of units

Assume you have the following data:

Table 23

Linear Regression
Example

X Values	Y Values
60	3.1
61	3.6
62	3.8
63	4.0
65	4.1

We are going to use a form of linear regression called "least squares", again there are many versions of linear regression, there are whole textbooks written on linear regression (I know because I actually took a one semester course where all we did was study different linear regression models) but this form is the most used, at least in my experience.

In "least squares" we are determining the slope and the intercept of the model in question (the B and the A). The following definitions are used in our analysis:

X and Y are the variables
B = slope of the regression line
A = The intercept point of the regression line and the y axis
N = Number of values or elements
X = X values (in this instance the units), the predictor
Y = The response being predicted
Sum X*Y = Sum of the product of X times Y
Sum X = Sum of the values of X
Sum Y = Sum of the values of Y
Sum X^2 = Sum of the squares of the X values

As usual we set up a table:

Table 24

Linear Regression
Example

X Values	Y Values	X*Y	X^2
60	3.1	186	3,600
61	3.6	220	3,721
62	3.8	236	3,844
63	4.0	252	3,969
65	4.1	267	4,225
311	18.6	1,160	19,359

The equations that determine the A and B values are:

B = [{N*Sum(X*Y)}-Sum(X)*Sum(Y)]/{(N*SumX^2)-(SumX)^2}
      Call this P   Call this Q
A = (SumY – B*(Sum X))/N

Call this R

As usual here is the step by step method of solving this

Solve P

N = 5

Sum X*Y = 1,160

Sum X = 311

Sum Y = 18.6

Sum X * Sum Y = 5,784.6

P = (5 *1,160)-5,884.6 = 13.9

Solve Q

N = 5

Sum X^2 = 19,359

(Sum X)^2 = 96,721

Q = (5*19,359) – 96,721= 74

B = P/Q = 13.9/74 = 0.19

Solve R

Sum Y = 18.6

B = 0.19

Sum X = 311

N = 5

R = {18.6-(0.19*3.11)}/5 = -8.098

Y = A + B X

Y = -8.098 + 0.19(X)

The final table shows how well our estimate was for our data set:

Table 25

Linear	B =	0.19

Regression

Example		A =		-8.098	Regression	
X Values	Y Values	X*Y	X^2		Estimate of Y	Delta
60	3.1	186	3,600		3.30	0.20
61	3.6	220	3,721		3.49	-0.11
62	3.8	236	3,844		3.68	-0.12
63	4.0	252	3,969		3.87	-0.13
65	4.1	267	4,225		4.25	0.15

There is also a value that can be calculated that is called the Correlation Coefficient (r). It is beyond the scope of this paper to show you how to calculate this value however it is easily done and you can look it up online. It measures the strength of the linear association between the X and Y values. It is always between -1 and 1. For this particular example the r value is about 0.92.

You will also see the term r Squared used in some instances, this is called the coefficient of determination. This measures the predictive ability of the linear regression model. In this case it is 0.92^2 = 0.84. The higher the value of r Squared the more comfortable you should feel with the predictions of the model.

There are a lot of assumptions that are inherent in the use of linear regression models. If you are doing a dissertation or something of that sort, you should investigate those assumptions and see how they impact your model. Usually for the purposes of cost projection, linear regression is fairly accurate as long as your r value is higher than 0.8. You should always chart the X and Y values of course to see what they look like. If they do not look linear then you are pretty well assured that the use of a linear equation would not work. Here is the data set above charted:

Chart 1

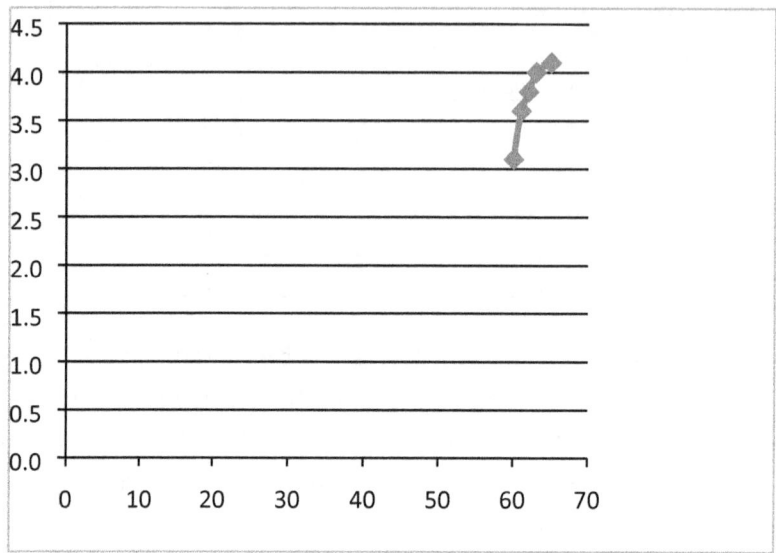

As you can see the values are approximately linear and therefore we had a good r value and therefore we should be able to predict our next value (66) based on this regression.

There are a few other things you should know just in case you get a hard core statistician doing the projections on some project. If you someone is performing multiple linear regression (more than one B value and more than one X value combined to give you a Y value) then the appropriate measures of effectiveness are adjusted r and adjusted r squared. This is important because the r values always increase in effectiveness when more polynomials are added. Make sure you do not think your projection is better than it really is.

Also, the Y value is usually called the dependent variable or the response variable. The X value is called the independent variable or the predictor variable.

10. Salvage Value

Salvage value is what is left at the end of the life cycle that has some useful value to the project. Salvage value is also known as residual value. There are numerous ways to calculate the salvage value, all of the methods will likely be wrong. The true salvage value is whatever the market will bear at the end of the life cycle. This is impossible to predict apriori. It is important to represent salvage value if you truly think there will be some value to the project because this can be a significant discriminator in the life cycle (especially when the life cycle is only a few years). You should always do a sensitivity analysis showing what the decision would be without the salvage value.

Here is an example of a Salvage value calculation:

Assume I have a 5 year life cycle, assume the first cost is $10,000 and I have a salvage value of $2,000. The appropriate discount rate is 3% midyear. What is the present value of the salvage value?

Again I will use a table to show the value.

Table 26

Year	First Cost	Salvage Value	Cash Flow	Discount	Present Value
0	($10,000)		($10,000)	1.0000	($10,000)
1			$0	0.9853	$0
2			$0	0.9566	$0
3			$0	0.9288	$0

4		$0	0.9017	$0
5	$2,000	$2,000	0.8755	$1,751
				($8,249)

The salvage value has reduced the cost of the life cycle by $1,751. This is 17.5% of the total. If there were many cost items then this 17.5% could be a significant factor in the life cycle. That is why it is very important to do a sensitivity analysis when you assume a salvage value because it is an assumption based on today's set of facts and those facts change.

How does one obtain an estimate of the salvage value? Often this value is derived based on an assumption of useful life of the item in the life cycle. Let's assume it is a truck and we assume the truck will last 6 years. The salvage value could be equal to the Kelly blue book projection of its value, it could also be equal to the MACRS value or the straight line depreciation value. None of these assumptions are right or wrong, because the true value is what you can get for the truck if you try to sell it (or what it would cost you to replace the truck).

The longer the life cycle the less impact the salvage value has on the final decision. Again, always do a sensitivity analysis and always state the basis of how you calculated the salvage value for any particular item under consideration in the life cycle.

11. Format for a life cycle cost analysis

The final format you decide will be highly dependent upon the audience that will be reviewing the life cycle. If you have, and it is usually the case, a mix of high and low understanding reviewers then I recommend the following:

A. Cover Sheet
B. Table of Contents
C. Executive Summary-Here you tell what your recommendations are.
D. Project Description-Describe the purpose of what the project is and what you hope to accomplish.
E. Alternative Description-Describe each alternative and the differences in the alternatives
F. Cost data-Describe each of the cost items that will be used in the report and in general how the values were developed
G. Calculations-Spreadsheets-Show the actual values calculated. Often a matrix of the calculations (say the final net present values) will suffice. Save the calculations themselves for an Appendix.
H. Interpretation and recommendation-If necessary describe how the data was interpreted, always provide a general recommendation based on the primary facts of the analysis.
I. Sensitivity analysis-Show how the change in values in certain variables will lead to a different decision. Often a matrix is useful here to show the decision point changes. Also include any intangibles that might influence the decision.
J. Appendices-Typically there will be at least one appendix showing the calculations that go into the analysis. Often there will be a second showing the data sources.

12. Inflation

Inflation is the general rise of prices over time. For life cycle analysis purposes two things should happen when you account for inflation. One you must make sure you have the appropriate inflation rate for each activity. Two you must make sure the discount rate is properly applied (when doing an analysis with inflation it is usually called a current dollar analysis). Here is an example of application of inflation and discounting.

Assume the following:

Inflation

Constant Discount Rate:	2.50%
General inflation:	3.00%
Total discount:	5.50%
Energy Differential:	1.50%
Total energy inflation:	4.50%

Table 27

Life Cycle Example including inflation:						
	First	Energy	O&M	Cash		Present
Year	Cost	Cost	Cost	Flow	Disc	Worth
0	$10,000			$10,000	1.0000	$10,000
1		$1,000	$1,000	$2,000	0.9736	$1,947
2		$1,045	$1,030	$2,075	0.9228	$1,915
3		$1,092	$1,061	$2,153	0.8747	$1,883
4		$1,141	$1,093	$2,234	0.8291	$1,852
5		$1,193	$1,126	$2,318	0.7859	$1,822

Now let's break this down to see what it is telling us:

The general discount rate (real rate, or constant rate) is 2.5%
The general inflation rate is 3.0%
That means the appropriate discount rate to use for all cash flows is 2.5% + 3.0% = 5.5 %

We have a differential escalation rate (this is typically given by the NIST tables) for energy of 1.5% which means that the Government believes energy will rise at 1.5% above general inflation over the next 5 years.

If the math has been done correctly that means that the energy escalation is 1.5% + 3.0% = 4.5%

General escalation for O&M is 3% per annum which means it is following the general inflation rate and therefore no additions to the general inflation rate is required.

After these factors have been applied then the life cycle sheet is just like any other life cycle.

It should make no difference whether you use a constant dollar or a current dollar analysis as far as who is the winner bidder (as mentioned earlier if A>B, then A*1.x>B*1.x) however it can affect the percentage of difference.

When one should use a current versus a constant dollar analysis is driven by the requirements of the life cycle. You should always use differential escalation regardless of constant versus current. Beyond that, it is really dependent on a lot of other factors as to which you need. Also, if you have any salvage values or replacement costs, those have to be appropriately handled if you use a current dollar analysis.

13. Equivalence of the use of Present Worth, Future Worth and Uniform annual cost

By far Present Worth or Present value is the criteria used to determine the best alternative among many. But there are other criteria used but they are all equivalent to Present Worth. The other most used parameter (in my experience) is future worth. If one does the math correctly it provides the same answer. Assume the following:

Present Worth: 30,000

Discount Rate: 3% per annum

Life Cycle periods: 10 years

What is the future worth?

First determine the total of the discount.

Table 29

Year	Discount	Uninv Discount
0	1	1
1	0.985329	1.014889
2	0.95663	1.045336
3	0.928767	1.076696
4	0.901716	1.108997
5	0.875452	1.142267
6	0.849954	1.176535
7	0.825198	1.211831
8	0.801163	1.248186
9	0.777828	1.285631
10	0.755173	1.3242

8.65721   Does not include year 0 discount

Future value = 1.3242* 30,000 = $39,726

In other words the present value times the compound value of the discount rate in year 10 (the future rate valuation point).

The other criteria used is uniform annual cost (or equivalent uniform annual cost). This is simply the present worth divided by the total discount rate:

=$30,000/8.65721 = $3,465

This is also called the levelized cost. It is the annual value of this cash flow. If you would discount $3,465 each year you should get a summary value of $30,000

Table 30

Year	Cash Flow	Discount	Present Worth
0	0	1	0
1	$3,465.32	0.985329	$3,414.48
2	$3,465.32	0.95663	$3,315.03
3	$3,465.32	0.928767	$3,218.48
4	$3,465.32	0.901716	$3,124.73
5	$3,465.32	0.875452	$3,033.72
6	$3,465.32	0.849954	$2,945.36
7	$3,465.32	0.825198	$2,859.57
8	$3,465.32	0.801163	$2,776.29
9	$3,465.32	0.777828	$2,695.42
10	$3,465.32	0.755173	$2,616.92
			$30,000.00

The usefulness of the uniform annual cost is that it can be used to determine the best alternative when there is unequal lives. Another way to handle unequal lives is to determine the lowest common denominator for the lives of the alternatives under consideration. This can be very cumbersome when there are many alternatives and I recommend you use uniform annual cost.

14. Sensitivity Analysis

After you have completed the life cycle you must perform a sensitivity analysis to determine how good your recommendation is. For instance, some decisions are very robust (geek speak for works for most situations), others are highly dependent upon some factor in the analysis. In order to determine just how robust the decision you are recommending truly is you should ensure the decision maker knows the parameters that govern the bounds of the decision. The classical way to do this is to perform a sensitivity analysis on each parameter and state how over what range the decision does not change.

Assume you have the following two alternatives. The question you wish to answer is: For each parameter what must change in order for me to be indifferent to the solution. In other words I am driving the difference between A and B to 0 and determining if that is likely to occur.

Table 31
X

Sensitivity Analysis
Discount   4.50%
Salvage: 20.00%
Inflation: 4.00%
Alt A
O&M
Cost $30,000
First
Cost: $100,000

	First	O&M	Salvage	Cash		Present
Year	Cost	Cost	Value	Flow	Disc	Worth
0	$100,000	$0	$0	$100,000	1.0000	$100,000
1	$0	$31,200	$0	$31,200	0.9782	$30,521

2	$0	$32,448	$0	$32,448	0.9361	$30,375
3	$0	$33,746	$0	$33,746	0.8958	$30,229
4	$0	$35,096	$0	$35,096	0.8572	$30,085
5	$0	$36,500	($20,000)	$16,500	0.8203	$13,535
					Total	$234,745

Alt B
O&M
Cost $40,000
First
Cost: $50,000

Year	First Cost	O&M Cost	Salvage Value	Cash Flow	Disc	Present Worth
0	$50,000	$0	$0	$50,000	1.0000	$50,000
1	$0	$41,600	$0	$41,600	0.9782	$40,694
2	$0	$43,264	$0	$43,264	0.9361	$40,500
3	$0	$44,995	$0	$44,995	0.8958	$40,306
4	$0	$46,794	$0	$46,794	0.8572	$40,113
5	$0	$48,666	($10,000)	$38,666	0.8203	$31,718
					Total	$243,331

Delta: **$8,587**

X
A is preferred to B

First I will determine what my parameters are: They are-
First Cost
O&M Cost
Salvage Value
Escalation
Discount

Note that each of these are a variable in my analysis.
Therefore if I change one it may have an impact on the

decision. The question to answer is at what point does my decision change or do I become indifferent.

What I wish to do is drive the Delta to 0, for each parameter. I change only one parameter at a time and do this for each parameter until I get a change. If I cannot obtain a 0 then the parameter is said to be dominant for the alternative it supports.

Starting with the first cost-At what point does the first cost have to rise for Alternative A or fall for Alternative B?

This spreadsheet shows the analysis. I chose to increase the First Cost for Alternative A and captured the increase as a percentage.

Table 32

Sensitivity Analysis for First Cost

Discoun				
t	4.50%			
Salvage:	20.00%			
Inflation				
:	4.00%			
Alt A				
O&M				
Cost	$30,000			
First	$115,41			110.27
Cost:	6	%inc		%

	First	O&M	Salvage	Cash		Present
Yea r	Cost	Cost	Value	Flow	Disc	Worth
0	$110,27 2	$0	$0	$110,27 2	1.0000	$110,27 2

Year	First Cost	O&M Cost	Salvage Value	Cash Flow	Disc	Present Worth
1	$0	$31,200	$0	$31,200	0.9782	$30,521
2	$0	$32,448	$0	$32,448	0.9361	$30,375
3	$0	$33,746	$0	$33,746	0.8958	$30,229
4	$0	$35,096	$0	$35,096	0.8572	$30,085
5	$0	$36,500	($22,054)	$14,445	0.8203	$11,849
					Total	$243,331

Alt B

O&M Cost $40,000

First Cost: $50,000

Year	First Cost	O&M Cost	Salvage Value	Cash Flow	Disc	Present Worth
0	$50,000	$0	$0	$50,000	1.0000	$50,000
1	$0	$41,600	$0	$41,600	0.9782	$40,694
2	$0	$43,264	$0	$43,264	0.9361	$40,500
3	$0	$44,995	$0	$44,995	0.8958	$40,306
4	$0	$46,794	$0	$46,794	0.8572	$40,113
5	$0	$48,666	($10,000)	$38,666	0.8203	$31,718
					Total	$243,331

Delta: $0

Thus the decision point is at about $110K or a 10% rise in the first cost of A before you are indifferent between A and B. The decision maker now has this piece of information, if my assumption on first cost is incorrect by less than 10% I have made a good decision.

Here is the final matrix

Table 33

	Change Value	Percent Change	
First Cost	$110,272	110.27%	
O&M Cost	31704.2	101.62%	
Inflation	-2.43%	- 164.47%	Requires deflation
Discount	10.80%	41.66%	Pretty much non repsonsive
Salvage	-$9,532	209.82%	

Here are the spreadsheets that supports the matrix.

Sensitivity Analysis for escalation
Discount   4.50%
Salvage: 20.00%
Inflation: -2.43%
Alt A
O&M
Cost $30,000
First
Cost: $100,000

	First Cost	O&M Cost	Salvage Value	Cash Flow	Disc	Present Worth
Year						
0	$100,000	$0	$0	$100,000	1.0000	$100,000
1	$0	$29,270	$0	$29,270	0.9782	$28,633
2	$0	$28,559	$0	$28,559	0.9361	$26,734

Year	First Cost	O&M Cost	Salvage Value	Cash Flow	Disc	Present Worth
3	$0	$27,864	$0	$27,864	0.8958	$24,960
4	$0	$27,186	$0	$27,186	0.8572	$23,305
5	$0	$26,525	($20,000)	$6,525	0.8203	$5,353
					Total	$208,985

Alt B
O&M Cost $40,000
First Cost: $50,000

	First	O&M	Salvage	Cash		Present
Year	Cost	Cost	Value	Flow	Disc	Worth
0	$50,000	$0	$0	$50,000	1.0000	$50,000
1	$0	$39,027	$0	$39,027	0.9782	$38,178
2	$0	$38,078	$0	$38,078	0.9361	$35,645
3	$0	$37,152	$0	$37,152	0.8958	$33,281
4	$0	$36,248	$0	$36,248	0.8572	$31,073
5	$0	$35,367	($10,000)	$25,367	0.8203	$20,809
					Total	$208,985

Delta: $0

Sensitivity Analysis for O&M
Discount 4.50%
Salvage: 20.00%
Inflation: 4.00%

Alt A
O&M Cost $31,704
First Cost: $100,000

	First	O&M	Salvage	Cash		Present
Year	Cost	Cost	Value	Flow	Disc	Worth

0	$100,000	$0	$0	$100,000	1.0000	$100,000
1	$0	$32,972	$0	$32,972	0.9782	$32,255
2	$0	$34,291	$0	$34,291	0.9361	$32,100
3	$0	$35,663	$0	$35,663	0.8958	$31,947
4	$0	$37,089	$0	$37,089	0.8572	$31,794
5	$0	$38,573	($20,000)	$18,573	0.8203	$15,236
					Total	$243,331

Alt B
O&M
Cost $40,000
First
Cost: $50,000

	First	O&M	Salvage	Cash		Present
Year	Cost	Cost	Value	Flow	Disc	Worth
0	$50,000	$0	$0	$50,000	1.0000	$50,000
1	$0	$41,600	$0	$41,600	0.9782	$40,694
2	$0	$43,264	$0	$43,264	0.9361	$40,500
3	$0	$44,995	$0	$44,995	0.8958	$40,306
4	$0	$46,794	$0	$46,794	0.8572	$40,113
5	$0	$48,666	($10,000)	$38,666	0.8203	$31,718
					Total	$243,331

Delta: **$0**

Sensitivity Analysis for Salvage Value
Discount   4.50%
Salvage: 20.00%
Inflation: 4.00%
Alt A
O&M
Cost $30,000
First
Cost: $100,000

Year	First Cost	O&M Cost	Salvage Value	Cash Flow	Disc	Present Worth
0	$100,000	$0	$0	$100,000	1.0000	$100,000
1	$0	$31,200	$0	$31,200	0.9782	$30,521
2	$0	$32,448	$0	$32,448	0.9361	$30,375
3	$0	$33,746	$0	$33,746	0.8958	$30,229
4	$0	$35,096	$0	$35,096	0.8572	$30,085
5	$0	$36,500	($9,532)	$26,968	0.8203	$22,122
					Total	$243,332

Alt B
O&M
Cost $40,000
First
Cost: $50,000

Year	First Cost	O&M Cost	Salvage Value	Cash Flow	Disc	Present Worth
0	$50,000	$0	$0	$50,000	1.0000	$50,000
1	$0	$41,600	$0	$41,600	0.9782	$40,694
2	$0	$43,264	$0	$43,264	0.9361	$40,500
3	$0	$44,995	$0	$44,995	0.8958	$40,306
4	$0	$46,794	$0	$46,794	0.8572	$40,113
5	$0	$48,666	($10,000)	$38,666	0.8203	$31,718
					Total	$243,331

Delta: $0

Sensitivity Analysis for discount
Discount   10.80%
Salvage: 20.00%
Inflation: 4.00%
Alt A
O&M
Cost $30,000
First $100,000

Cost:

Year	First Cost	O&M Cost	Salvage Value	Cash Flow	Disc	Present Worth
0	$100,000	$0	$0	$100,000	1.0000	$100,000
1	$0	$31,200	$0	$31,200	0.9500	$29,640
2	$0	$32,448	$0	$32,448	0.8574	$27,821
3	$0	$33,746	$0	$33,746	0.7738	$26,113
4	$0	$35,096	$0	$35,096	0.6984	$24,510
5	$0	$36,500	($20,000)	$16,500	0.6303	$10,400
					Total	$218,485

Alt B
O&M
Cost $40,000
First
Cost: $50,000

Year	First Cost	O&M Cost	Salvage Value	Cash Flow	Disc	Present Worth
0	$50,000	$0	$0	$50,000	1.0000	$50,000
1	$0	$41,600	$0	$41,600	0.9500	$39,520
2	$0	$43,264	$0	$43,264	0.8574	$37,095
3	$0	$44,995	$0	$44,995	0.7738	$34,818
4	$0	$46,794	$0	$46,794	0.6984	$32,681
5	$0	$48,666	($10,000)	$38,666	0.6303	$24,372
					Total	$218,485

Delta: **$0**

15. Wrap up

The take aways from this course are the following:

a. Life cycle is all about relative values between the alternatives under investigation. If there is only one alternative then no life cycle is required.
b. Life cycle determines the most cost effective use of funds based on a pre determined value for those funds (discount rate) over a certain period of time.
c. If I have done the math correctly I will always have the same winner whether I do life cycle in present value, or future value or Uniform annual cost.
d. A discounted payback and a discounted SIR is more accurate than a non-discounted SIR or payback.
e. Be careful when using Internal Rate of Return for a decision.
f. Life Cycle is all about determining if the initial first cost is off set by savings later on in the life of the system. If it is not then the high first cost is not justified.
g. Sensitivity analysis is required for all life cycles in order to show just how effective the decision is over a the data set that makes up the components of the decision.
h. Life Cycle Analysis is fun and easy (okay, I made that one up).